T4T

Cover art: Ellis Chase, "T4T" and "interlocking carabiners"
Cover design: Diana Baltog
Interior design: Brianna Chapman
Editor: Eliza Carlson
Publisher: Allison Blevins
Executive Editor: Kristiane Weeks-Rogers
Managing Editor: Bianca Dagostino

T4T
Evelyn Berry
ISBN 978-1-957248-66-0
Harbor Editions,
an imprint of Small Harbor Publishing

T4T

Evelyn Berry

Harbor Editions
Small Harbor Publishing

For Alex and Zoe

Contents

T4T

transsexual confessional

i forget my own monstrosity
until someone reminds me
they'll rubberneck my funeral
to sherlock my birth sex.

you get used to it,
the staring, when starring
in your own 24-7 sitcom.
the too-loud whisper, the obvious
gesture, the prying question.

i could try to play along, the useable suspect,
moonlight as hermaphrodite hermit
haunting the wet dreams of legislators.

could tell them the names my lover calls me,
what they write on my body in impermanent ink,

how my mother balks at the bawdy-slick
songs i whistle true as a godwit.

could deliver the rehearsed plea, a past drafted
for palatable consumption. but i won't give them that.

won't tell how panic
fangs my brain, frieze
calligraphed with tragic stories
of how uncertainty and shame beget death.

i know how a girl like me
becomes a cautionary tale
we recite to help each other survive.

no. i won't flaunt the wound to prove i'm alive.

self-portrait as nothing

before i was named
close to a real man
i performed my lack
black hole blank spot gone
not light of dead stars
tampered crime scene of
obscured memory
gendered antiquity
forgotten trinket
i pretend sparkle
abandon glitter
search for me back then

woman i was not
easily definable
like a numb throat
splatter ink blot splotch
in the space between
this empty body
post-obsolete sex
in pre-op junk shops
mistaken ornate
in lieu of good light
for shades of the dark
you'll find me missing

AFAB (Assigned Fairy at Birth)

faggotry found me young
yet unprepared.
i talked with a lisp,
swished my hips
when walking.
in the mirror, modeled
mother's earrings.

never passed
as a believable man— too femme,
too buoyant, splintered by boyhood,
no boundaries between secrets and shame.

in my they/them era, i wore a beard
doused in cheap glitter and desperation,
thrifted floral skirts,
plastic flower crowns.

i tell you this to suggest my queerness
did not bloom with hormones. i've always
been this fabulous and dangerous fairy,

queen mab's favorite son,
the name i stole still lingering
on the tip of your tongue.

Country Queers

in the tick-riddled fields beyond the creek,
where we skip stones, trade spit and nostalgia,
we make of our queer bodies a concert,
cricket choir fiddling their legs at dusk.

bullfrogs from the bog join in, all caught up
in backwoods cacophony. cicadas
sing like a frottoir, washboard steel-scrap-scraped,
guitar twang-tuned to match our crooked mouths.

i've known this home since before i was grown.
i'm leaving, but not until tomorrow.
here, we are moon-luminous and constant
as the night's sharp appetite for music.

we shed our dead names like rattlesnake skin.
we pretend our freckles honeysuckle.

in praise of your belly button

the point of origin, original
indent, the body's subtle, sudden-born
hint that we need one another to live.
tell me how all of this started, quiet,

our names not yet our names to abandon.
do you remember the first time i sank
my teeth into the soft of your belly,
lost in the wild-tossed riptide of impulse?

do you remember the first time you said
your own name out loud, the sting of gladness?
let us begin again, sinless in bliss,
mouths inventing new words for the sharp scent

of home. consecrated, hollow, holy,
hallowed and concave: your first provenance.

in praise of being fat

who names this sin, to love my fat body?
let me praise where i've been, this lived-in skin.

my belly sings a ballad ripening,
an abundant garden gorgon-gorgeous.

if i must be myth-monstrous, i'll sharpen
my teeth. i'll rewrite the story myself.

i'm transexual orpheus of smut,
orifice with an oral fixation.

fill my mouth with grease, chocolate, feast of
chubby thighs, thick calves, spit & cum & sweat.

i'll regret nothing, not red dress excess,
not afternoon sex in a king-sized bed,

my loves, their bodies like mine, intertwined.
we are laughing & fat & hot as fuck.

discipline

when you swing swift, open palm, to pinken
my upturned ass, i brace for the soft sting.
i take a sharp breath, then the ache stills me.
your hands remind me to whom i belong.

you grasp my long hair, pull taut to tame me,
snare a whimper until i gasp your name.
give me this reverie, animal urged
to break free. break me. i beg, *please, don't stop*.

i lose count and collapse, still obeisant
in your embrace. you caress where you've bruised,
where you've used skin to mark me your canvas.
you coax me back from the brink of spent sense,

call me *good girl*, your leather-leashed darling.
i promise, i'll be a good girl this time.

easy worship

you tease me for my love of your armpits,
which you haven't shaved for four years.
but i also adore your collarbone,
your strong calves, your shoulders,
your hips dipping beneath
your soft belly's lush folds,
where sometimes i lick
sweat as if droughted.

i am wet
for every inch of you.

self-portrait as strawberry

it is in your mouth i come to become.
i was born to be plucked ripe and swallowed,
crushed red in your teeth, honeysuckle-bled,
sucked until sated, not fated to rot
on the vine, another sugar-ruined

                        fruit.
                        tart-pulped seed spiller.
                        blessed five-star sinner.

let me stain your tongue ruby-lush, strawberry bruise, a
new communion of fat flesh, the succor of a chubby
transsexual's plump belly, cheeks cherry-flushed, blush-
burned. i am abundant as fuck, like fruit weighing the
branches on the tree of knowledge!

i am revived with delight, wild and bursting!
spit me,
bury me,
tamp the damp
dirt flat.
let me return,
your faggot fragaria.

what survives you must feed back to the earth.

aubade with constraints

the body stays still when it's touched– good slut–
broken at the break of light-sundered dawn.
sensation already gone when tied down,
absence erratic to be stuffed, stretched, glut.

the body obeys its own gravity
when wrist-cuffed, lust-lashed, its feral gnash-bite
muzzle-muffled, pinned beneath your muscles,
its name soon lost in search of salt-salvage.

the body betrays its feral-wreck want,
girldick buzzed into clitoral pleasure,
sudden throb of becoming something new.
you wait until it begs, wretched and edged.

the body a blade of vexed appetite
when you never let it finish, a cage
for its endless hunger. what a good girl,
you tell her, coaxing her back to herself.

the girl slips herself from the restraints,
embraces you, thanks you for the ache.

personal brand

i'm only a slut on the internet
where desire is hypothetical.
online, i aim to be mysterious.

no one even knows my name. *scorpio*,
i write in my tinder bio. kidding–
i was banned for being transsexual.

i'm plagued by the common concerns: dying,
for one. or dying alone. or dying
with so much housework left still unfinished.

like most failures my age, i was smart once.
i had potential or at least something
akin to intuition: clarity,

purpose, a future of endless promise
ahead. i've spent ten years drunk on the past.
i'm a sucker for nostalgia's switchblade.

i watch another youtube video
about discontinued tamagotchis.
let's repackage art as viral content.

tbh, doom-scrolling's a great pastime,
though maybe algorithms don't love me.
won't you fallow me and lick my stratus?

i've been thinking of using gofundme
to crowdfund tit implants or maybe rent.
sorry, i spent fellowships on hormones.

i will practice domestic normalcy.
the usual polite conversations:
the cost of eggs, apocalypse weather,

fascism, the loss of community.
at the river's edge, on half-eroded
stones, moss grows without applause.

the decoy

after John Collier

to be painted femme fatale, condemned fatal:
a woman's beauty is a dangerous deception
in the hands of a man who demands
to own her like a plucked rose.

let me be the decoy instead,
damsel in undress, glinting
luminescent like a knife
bound to my ankle.

ugh!

after Jane Schoenbrun

dysphoria-dazed, i refused to face
my face in the mirror– favorite haunt.
ugh, how miserable to have a body.

i imagined myself a flightless bird
whose song had been stripped from morning's chorus.
dysphoria-dazed, i refused to voice

what is so obvious now. *Change Your Life,*
rilke commanded; i didn't listen.
ugh, how miserable to have a body.

before i was reborn transsexual,
yes, i buried myself. suffocated.
dysphoria-dazed, i refused to live

longer in that strange, static-echo world.
there is still time. change your life, your body.
dysphoria: days spent wasted saying,
ugh, how miserable to have a body.

self-portrait as south carolina peach

we spent summer nights at the drive-in,
necking in truck beds, mosquitos
blood-snacking on our bare thighs.
we came home late, bite-marked.
the first time i bruised,
i admired skin
turning dark
like a
fruit.

once,
i puked
a bottle
of pills into
the toilet, fled class and
collapsed on tiled floor. once,
a girl offered to brighten
my blood. she pressed her lips to flesh.
i was still soft enough to ruin.

the pollution started young, high on
anything i could scavenge from
medicine cabinets. frost
pummeled the peach orchards
that year i lost
to the kick
of brief
bliss.

how
did i
live like this?
the memories
decadence-decayed.
i just wanted to feel
present, like how, as a child,
i'd eat peaches in the backyard,
nectar grown from the same dirt as me.

high-risk behavior

after the second eviction notice,
i scrounge for something to sell:
weathered textbooks, derelict t-shirts,

antique penny worth ten bucks. blood.
at the clinic, i don't bother to lie
on the questionnaire, say plain my brand of wreck:

pills, booze, bareback, reckless ruin
strewn through my veins like locusts left dead
after feeding on pesticide's harvest.

my doctor tells me my blood's suspect,
possible pestilence, implicit threat.
the body's troubled crucible brews disease.

i'm released back into winter morning
and exhale hot into my blistered hands
still empty of anything that can keep me alive.

self-portrait at nineteen

all summer, i worked shifts at old navy
& snorted molly from an iphone screen
in the backseat of a car parked nowhere,
a happy heathen not yet grief-plundered.

once, i was a boy unafraid to die.
i would swallow almost anything meant
to kill me if, at first, it got me high:
pills left over from surgery pilfered

from my parents' medicine cabinet,
coffee cups of dark liquor, gas station
feasts, bounty of grease, sugar, cigarettes.
how else to parachute from the body?

aliveness, this useless extravagance
i have wasted once before, but no more.

AMAB (Assigned Mary at Birth)

don't worry, i was socialized faggot,
good judge judy of character, harmless
as your gay best friend, barely a real dyke.
i'm your mary, your cunt fairy, rarely
hot enough to steal your man. call me slay,
boots pussy the house down, yass-queened with slang
straight white women learned from gay men who learned
from black trans women. when your boyfriend asks,
i can pass fairly fish in the right light.
let me be your favorite queerbait, brick,
line, stinker. benign as a brain tumor,
designed for your comfort, false femme severed
from real womanhood. sorry, i brought up
politics while we were watching drag race.

i turn off my phone for self-care but history keeps happening

while i'm logged off, a new hashtag:
this time a transfemme, beaten to death.
someone tweets her two-week-old selfie
screen-shot from her instagram feed
flooded now with incantations of her name.

scroll away to find someone has tweeted about the new
bill in texas. someone tweets about the new bill in georgia.
someone tweets, *235 anti-trans bills have been proposed across
the country.* someone tweets about the new bill in south
carolina. someone tweets, *i'm really scared to live here.*
someone tweets about the new bill in kentucky. someone
tweets, *322 anti-trans bills have been proposed across the country.*
someone tweets about the new bill in tennessee. someone
tweets about the new bill in arkansas.

this bill will charge trans people as sexual offenders if
they use the bathroom in public. & this bill will restrict
trans teens from accessing puberty blockers. & this bill
will restrict trans adults up to the age of 21 from
accessing gender-related healthcare. & this bill will restrict
trans adults up to the age of 26 from accessing gender-
affirming healthcare. & this bill will restrict trans adults
from accessing gender-affirming healthcare. & this bill
will rename gender-affirming healthcare as child abuse. &
this bill will out trans students to their parents. & this bill
will not allow teachers to use a student's chosen name. &
this bill will remove trans people from sports. & this bill
will remove trans kids from their parents' care. & this bill
will remove kids from their trans parents' care. & this bill

will remove the word "trans" from the classroom. & this bill will remove trans stories from the public library. & this bill will remove trans people from public life.

this bill will remove trans people.

someone tweets, *#eradicatetransgenderism.*

someone tweets, *the problem with trans people is that they're just looking for attention.*
someone tweets, *is anyone paying attention?*

someone retweets an article from the new york times about the flaws of trans healthcare, which includes no interviews with trans people. someone tweets a selfie of the trans flight attendant who killed herself last week. someone tweets a video of a drag brunch protest, twelve men armed with semi-automatics. someone tweets a picture of a celebrity trans actor with a bullet hole photoshopped into his head. someone tweets, *the problem with trans people is that they're always trying to force it down everyone's throat.* someone tweets a meme about teaching their 2-year-old son how to be a real man. someone tweets about a father who says, *if my son came out as gay, i'd kill him.* someone tweets, *i'm scared to come out to my dad because i don't know if he'll ever speak to me again.* someone tweets, *over 515 anti-trans bills have been proposed across the country.*

someone tweets, *kill yourself, kill yourself, kill yourself* on my selfie,
& i delete the replies before anyone else can see. i delete the selfie too.

someone tweets, *log off*, so i do.

but then someone tweets, *i feel like i'm shouting into the void, because the void keeps having panic attacks when they read the news and has logged offline.* someone tweets, *do you prefer the term transgender or transsexual?* someone tweets, *who cares? they're killing us.*

someone tweets about the young trans girl who killed herself two weeks ago. someone tweets a link to her suicide note, & i read it at 4am when i can't sleep. her suicide note details how her parents forced to detransition. someone tweets, *if you're reading this, please don't give up. don't give up just yet please.* someone tweets, *stay safe.* someone tweets, *please seek help. please don't do this.* someone tweets, *you deserved better.* someone tweets, *my heart breaks for you.* someone tweets, *please don't be gone. please.* someone replies, *get over it, he's dead.* someone replies, *cry about it, tranny.* someone tweets, *please still be alive.* someone tweets, *you are loved.*

her suicide note gets 66,000 likes and 7,532 retweets.

someone tweets, *hashtag hashtag hashtag.*
someone tweets, *the problem with trans people is they have the audacity to stay alive.*

someone tweets, *the problem with trans people is. the problem with trans people is.*
someone tweets, *the problem is trans people.*

someone tweets a link to an online hrt pharmacy, says, *get ready for the worst.* someone tweets, *get ready for what's coming.* someone tweets, *how am i supposed to buy groceries and go to work & go to school & keep going when i know there are people at the state house debating my existence?* someone tweets, *how am i supposed to go on?* someone tweets about how brave i am, again someone tweets, *i'm so tired of being brave. i just want to be safe.* someone tweets, *what we need right now, more than ever, is trans joy.* someone tweets a selfie of them kissing their trans girlfriend. someone tweets a photo of two trans men swimming in the ocean, publicly shirtless for the first time after their top surgery scars have healed. someone tweets a meme about a stuffed shark at ikea. someone tweets, *how's my progress? 3 years on t.* someone tweets, *i thought we were making progress. what happened?* someone tweets, *goodbye im sorry i just cant do it anymore.*

i wake to a new hashtag, and this time i'm afraid to read her name.

TDOR

remembrance, by which i mean reverence,
silence in lieu of your presence, your voice,
your chorus, your hand in mine, your kindness,
your joy— evidence that you were here once.

remembrance, by which i mean this language
is our grief's insufficient translation.
let me howl, let my body thrash, reject
this violent inheritance of ash.

let us live not just in shared memory.
let us tell another story, a song
that keeps us here, breathing, alive, and safe.
swear, stay here with me tomorrow, tonight.

let us recite, with care rather than shame:
your name, your name, your name, your name, your name.

prodigal daughter

what i know of sin, i learned in the sty
amid the swine, slurped mud and called it wine.
femme-fouled boy, faggot-spoiled sacrifice
offered at the altar and abandoned.

forgive my reckless want, lord, to belong
as more than soiled sacrament, fat sow
knife-split to gorge the prophets of gendered
violence. prayer, in their hands, a blade.

what do i know of penitence, patience,
except once the lord sent frenzied demons
into a drove of blameless pigs to drown?
how did we decide which beast to slaughter?

lord, i too am an impure animal.
i left home a son, return a daughter.

the book of evie

begotten, beget of, et cetera.
we're all yet beholden to being born.
i came out backwards (upside down, i guess,
like peter's inverted martyrdom).

trans is to tell a story in reverse:
revision, erasure and renaming
until the beginning's blurry enough
to believe. i'm uninterested, true,

in biological assignment. yes,
i can change sex easy as the lord turns
water into wine, by which i mean, no,
it's not easy. call it revelation,

the kind of daily marvel for which saints
once spent their whole lives praying to witness.

tease

i never turn down a free beer.
flirt with anyone with a wolf cut.
show off my freckles in dresses
that drop off my shoulders.
i want to be desired, don't you?
don't you know everyone
you've ever met is gonna die?
kiss me, don't stop, please.
remind me i'm still here.

in praise of drag kings

mascara-stippled stubble smeared
in the lesbian bar's harsh light,
thrusting to springsteen's
"dancing in the dark."

praise drag kings who spark
desire with a look or touch
or cocky grin when they catch eyes
with a sighing girl waving a dollar
over her head like a flag of surrender.

praise drag kings whose masc splendor
render us knee-weak and wanting,
boasting charm and technique
then disarm us with camp gags,
leaving us gasping with laughter.

praise drag kings who, like dandies,
don top hats, wear stylish
violet suits, and tap dance to cabaret tunes.

praise drags kings who croon
franki valli, bobbing gel-slick
pompadours: "can't keep
my eyes off of you."

praise drag kings in denim blue
and cowboy hats, bedazzled
boots scootin' to blues ballads

and honkey-tonk:
save a horse, ride a drag king!

praise drag kings leather-harnessed,
wearing nothing but sweat
and binding tape, reshaping
the landscape of machismo.

praise drag kings who have shown
us that masculinity is more
than toxic stereotypes, but rather
a gorgeous queer possibility.

february: south carolina

after James Wright

in the backyard, we slip
off our shirts, lean back
in the hammock.
we marvel at how
our bodies keep changing,
our breasts & bellies
slathered in cheap sun lotion,
the kind with sparkles.
i scrape glitter
from your skin
with my teeth.
we are feral
together, topless
& gently sun-pinked.
we sink into afternoon's
warm promise & pledge
to waste our lives like this,
floating just a few inches
above the earth.

T4T

because when my partner / undresses for the first time /
i'm undone / i'm envious of their earrings / biting their
lobes / they spread their legs, & i gasp / i have fasted for
more than a year / but here, right now, i feast / their hand
guides my head / i swallow them whole / their clit
overflows the fountain in me / i empty of any language /
that is not their name / i am wet as a last-penny wish / let
me drown here

because when i touch a body like mine / i trace familiar
lines / fingers on my girlfriend's throat, her back / bent
into crumpled bed sheets / we meet in erotic symmetry /
linger close, graze / skin, we tease, ease closer / i teach
her to be a good girl / like me / i lick cum from her belly

because mtf4ftm / mtf4nb / mtf4mtf / mtf4nb4mtf /
the ways we codify desire

because once, after sex, i pluck casey plett from a lover's
bookcase / the novel gifted by their california girlfriend /
that's a word we don't use / yet / we're low commitment,
casual / until the night in the hospital / the nurse asks
how they know me, why i'm there / holding their hand as
the anesthesia kicks in

because i run into my ex-boyfriend's / boyfriend at the
bar / he's read my book / he's six months on t / he tells
me about the first shot, how his boyfriend / administered
hormones in his thigh, a syringe pulled / secreted in a
bedside drawer / where once i stored my cpap / this, how

we share ourselves / share meds / share beds / share secret shames whispered / after taking too many shots of tequila

because trans people ask / questions about my life / besides / why?

because when i see another doll in public / there's a fugitive recognition / we acknowledge and don't acknowledge / we say / i like your hair / i like your dress / i like the way you know something / about who i am / without me asking / i like how / you don't ask / we're like sleeper agents / pronouncing words in a language / not spoken to another / in decades

because when i met my girlfriend / i didn't know right away / we sat next to each other / at dinner / for a friend leaving town / she kept dropping hints / until she told me / she too gave away / her good flannels to transmascs / and how she later regretted her charity / when she came out as a dyke

because maybe we're all slow to connect the dots / to construct some version of ourselves / that makes sense / of scattered notions of gender / trans once a word i avoided / & now a title i aim to gift / to anyone / who needs a way / to talk about how language mangles / their body in translation

because i feel / for maybe the first time / a sense of desperate familiarity / when i read the forums / when i read *nevada* / when i read archived zines / when i join the group chat / when i listen hard to stories that mirror mine

because sometimes, when trans women are in public together / we're more visible / to those who might harm us / and sometimes / i wonder who is looking / wondering / if we are like them / if they too might be happy, laughing, comfortable / like this

because i wouldn't know how to explain / to someone new / that i startle / when a balloon pops / because i've spent too many nights / reading obituaries / & news stories / i worry what the bouncer will say / when he sees the wrong sex on my id / what if someone clocks me? / what if it's someone with a gun?

because i've been in enough support groups / to know it is a miracle / every time / a trans person emerges / from that first year / alive

because once / my spouse told me / i'll love you / no matter what your body becomes / they tell me / your body becomes more gorgeous every day / your body belongs to you / you belong to me / you belong with me

because the first night / i met my spouse / they knew / they tied my hair in a ponytail / i'd been growing it out for two years / they called me pretty / i blushed / strawberry ripening red because when i come out / to my parents at o'charleys / on a monday night / the waitress asks / what will the birthday girl have? / my partner squeezes my hand and doesn't let go / because i'm scared to be seen so plainly by strangers / my family / friends / coworkers / when i tell my parents / i can't stop sobbing / long enough / to explain myself / they tell me / we know

because we reimagine / family as a coven / make out of our bodies / a kind of magic / that transforms even the most brutal / beautiful landscape / into home

because the space that feels safe is no place / it is people who know my name / is mine / to choose

stay here

an arietta for transfemmes

i love your voice, love your bright noise, your hands,
i rejoice in your perfect mascara,

glory your regret, that familiar wound,
a harmony you keep out of habit.

love your brittle, love your battle-weary,
love your fury, your grit, your gnashing heart,

love your kiss-tipsy laugh-snort, love you here,
love you safe, love you more than everything.

sister, let's praise that ordinary ache.
don't mistake flowers for funeral wreaths.

you must breathe a little longer– stay here.
love you tender as a lipstick-stained ear.

you will resist the gilded casket's grasp,
and let go of the past, restless with ghosts.

may the stories of how you've lived outlast
every elegy born from your mourning.

let us pray against storms another year
we'll spend not leaving each other behind.

you find your way back to yourself instead.
let them learn your name before you are dead.

love your name, love the way you say it slow,
like a word you invented, language forged

for your mouth. love your voice, did i tell you?
tomorrow, let me hear your voice again.

Acknowledgements

This chapbook was written with generous support from the South Carolina Arts Commission through their Individual Artist Fellowship for Poetry.

This chapbook was revised during a one-week writing residency at Firefly Farms, made possible by Sundress Academy for the Arts.

Thank you to my partners and friends, who agreed to share intimate stories in these poems.

Thank you to Allison Blevins, who first shared her enthusiasm for the project, Dustin Brookshire for your moral support, and Kristiane K. Weeks-Rogers and Eliza Carlson for your editorial eye and support.

Several of the poems in this chapbook previously appeared in publications or were written for performance, sometimes under different titles:

"AFAB" and "AMAB" were originally published in *The Journal*.

"Country Queers" and "High-Risk Behavior" were originally published in *Sandhills Magazine*.

"Discipline" was originally published in *Moist Poetry Journal*.

"Easy Worship" was originally published in *Horns, Volume III*.

"February: South Carolina" was originally published in *Day Job Journal*.

"I Turn Off My Phone for Self-Care But History Keeps Happening" was originally published in *otherwor(l)ds*.

"In Praise of Drag Kings" was originally published in *Queer Joy Zine*.

"In Praise of Your Belly Button" was originally published in *Meow Meow Pow Lit*.

"Prodigal Daughter," "Self-Portrait at Nineteen," and "The Decoy" were originally published in *Jasper Magazine Online*.

"Stay Here, An Arietta for Transfemmes" was originally written for *Singers & Stanzas*, a production of HALO (Holy City Arts & Lyric Opera), during which the poem was composed as an operatic art song by Laura Jobin-Acosta and debuted by singer Lindsay Metzger and pianist Isaac Hayward. An excerpt of the poem was selected as a Button Poetry Short Form Contest winner in Fall 2024.

"T4T" and "self-portrait as nothing" were originally published in *The Normal School*.

"Tease" was originally published in *Ballast Journal*.

"TDOR" was written and performed during Trans Day of Remembrance 2024 at the SC Statehouse.

"Ugh!" was originally published in *fairglow*, an anthology of writing based on the films of Jane Schoenbrun.

Evelyn Berry is an angry, horny, sad, transsexual, Southern poet, performer, editor, and educator living in South Carolina. She's the author of *Grief Slut* (Sundress Publications, 2024) the chapbook *Buggery* (Bateau Press, 2020).

She is the recipient of the National Endowment for the Arts Poetry Fellowship and South Carolina Arts Commission Individual Artist Fellowship for Poetry. She is the winner of the BOOM Chapbook Prize, Button Poetry Short Form Contest, Dr. Linda Veldheer Memorial Prize, KAKALAK Poetry Prize, Emrys Poetry Prize, Broad River Prize for Prose, and other honors. H

Her work has appeared in dozens of journals, including *Beloit Poetry Journal, The Normal School, Moist Poetry Journal, Gigantic Sequins, The Journal, Taco Bell Quarterly*, and elsewhere.

Learn more at EvelynBerryWriter.com.

About Small Harbor Publishing

Small Harbor Publishing is a 501c3 nonprofit organization. Our goal is to publish unique and diverse voices. We are a feminist press, and we are committed to diversity and inclusion. We strive to bring new voices to a devoted and expanding readership.

Small Harbor Publishing began in 2018 with the first issue of *Harbor Review*. The magazine is an online space where poetry and art converse. *Harbor Review* quickly grew and now publishes reviews and runs multiple micro chapbook competitions, including the Washburn Prize and the Editor's Prize.

In July 2020, Small Harbor Publishing was officially incorporated and began Harbor Editions. Harbor Editions accepts submissions through a chapbook open reading period, a hybrid chapbook open reading period, the Marginalia Series, and the Laureate Prize.

In 2023, Harbor Anthologies began with a mission to promote texts that explore social justice issues and highlight marginalized writers.

If you would like to support Small Harbor Publishing, visit our "About" page at: smallharborpublishing.com/about.